Original title:
Mottled Hints Beyond the Elf Shuck

Copyright © 2025 Swan Charm
All rights reserved.

Author: Kaido Väinamäe
ISBN HARDBACK: 978-1-80559-451-2
ISBN PAPERBACK: 978-1-80559-950-0

Tales Carried by the Weight of Gnarled Branches

Whispers of the forest sigh,
In shadows deep where secrets lie.
Gnarled branches stretch and bend,
Guardians of tales that never end.

Upon the bark, the stories weave,
Of lovers lost and dreams that grieve.
Each twist and knot a page turned,
In nature's book, wisdom earned.

Fog drapes low in morning's gold,
Wrapped in tales of the brave and bold.
Roots tangled deep in ancient ground,
Echoes of voices still resound.

Time flows slow through silent woods,
Breath of life in tranquil moods.
Boughs like arms around the frail,
Bearing witness to every tale.

So listen close, the whispers call,
Of laughter, love, and gentle fall.
In gnarled branches, hearts will mend,
The forest keeps us till the end.

The Dance of Color in Sylvan Thoughts

Beneath the canopy so wide,
Colors dance as shadows glide.
Leaves of crimson, gold, and green,
In harmony, a vibrant scene.

Sunlight filters, casting dreams,
Rippling through in golden beams.
Each petal sways to nature's song,
In the forest where we belong.

Mossy stones and streams that gleam,
Nature flows like a timeless dream.
Rustling whispers through the air,
A gentle touch, a fleeting prayer.

The wind carries hues so bright,
Painting the day, igniting night.
In sylvan thoughts, our spirits soar,
We dance again forevermore.

As the seasons paint their tale,
Nature's brush will never fail.
In every shade, our hearts will sway,
Lost in color's pure ballet.

Whispers of Enchanted Shade

Beneath a bough, the silence sighs,
Where emerald leaves catch dreamy skies.
The fae dance lightly, hearts aglow,
In twilight's warmth, their secrets flow.

Murmering streams weave tales of old,
As ancient trees their stories hold.
Each rustling leaf, a whispered prayer,
In the enchanted shade, magic's flair.

A gentle breeze, a lover's touch,
Awakens dreams that mean so much.
In every shadow, a spark ignites,
Guiding lost souls through starry nights.

Moonbeams filter through branches wide,
Painting pathways where hopes reside.
In the heart of the darkened wood,
Whispers of wonder softly mood.

Here time stands still, the world fades away,
In the enchanted shade, we long to stay.
For every sigh holds a hidden spell,
In twilight's embrace, all is well.

Starlit Secrets in the Thicket

In the depths where shadows creep,
Secrets linger, silence deep.
Beneath the stars, the thicket glows,
Hiding wonders that no one knows.

Rustling leaves above my head,
Whisper stories long since said.
Each constellation tells a tale,
Of dreams that in the night prevail.

Footsteps soft on moonlit ground,
In this sanctuary, peace is found.
Through tangled vines, the pathways wind,
A treasure trove for the seeking mind.

A hush envelops earth and skies,
As twilight falls, the magic rises.
In the stillness, hearts align,
In starlit secrets, love entwines.

Echoing laughter, the night unfolds,
Stories of the brave and bold.
In thickets thick with shaded grace,
We find our dreams, our sacred space.

Echoes of the Glimmering Grove

In a grove where the ferns grow high,
Whispers dance and shadows fly.
Glimmers twinkle in the night,
An invitation to take flight.

Echoes of laughter fill the air,
A symphony of joy laid bare.
Beneath the stars, a path unfolds,
Woven with threads of ancient gold.

Moonlit beams on dew-kissed grass,
Create a magic, unsurpassed.
Every step, an echo's call,
In the grove, we feel it all.

To wander here is to be free,
To lose oneself and simply be.
In the glimmering glow of night,
Hearts unite, the world feels right.

The air is thick with dreams untold,
In the grove where legends hold.
With each whisper, time flows on,
In echoes sweet, we are reborn.

Chasing Shadows Among Sapphire Foliage

Through sapphire leaves, the sunlight weaves,
Chasing shadows where the heart believes.
Every corner holds a spark,
A hidden story in the dark.

The rustling branches call my name,
In the dance of light, I join the game.
With every step, I seek to find,
The whispers lost, to fate aligned.

Cool breezes carry scents so sweet,
Among the foliage, my heart skips a beat.
The world awaits, a tapestry bright,
In the colors of day and the cloak of night.

Moments linger, then drift away,
As I chase shadows that brightly sway.
In the heart of green, my spirit soars,
Unlocking dreams through hidden doors.

In nature's embrace, we come alive,
Each shadow chased helps us thrive.
Under sapphire skies, together we roam,
In the wild's heart, we find our home.

Veiled Murmurs of the Wandering Breeze

In whispered tones, the willows sway,
Carrying secrets of yesterday.
They dance with joy, a playful tone,
Nature's voice, softly sown.

Among the leaves, a story weaves,
Of hidden dreams and gentle grieves.
Each ripple sings, a tale untold,
In the arms of the night, so bold.

Through valleys deep, the shadows roam,
Echoing whispers of their home.
A wistful sigh, as stars align,
The breeze brings warmth, sweet as wine.

The moonlight glows, a silken thread,
Guiding souls through paths of dread.
In every turn, an echo stays,
Veiled murmurs of forgotten days.

So pause awhile, let nature speak,
In every hush, a truth to seek.
For in the stillness, life reveals,
The wandering breeze, the heart it steals.

Beneath the Bark, Secrets Lie

In the rough embrace of ancient trees,
Whispers linger in every breeze.
Beneath the bark, life swirls away,
Silent murmurs where shadows play.

Crimson leaves and emerald hues,
Hold the tales that time accrues.
In knotted roots, of love and strife,
The heartbeat echoes, the pulse of life.

Tiny creatures, a world unseen,
Dancing through woods, serene, serene.
They weave their spells in soil so rich,
In every nook, an unseen stitch.

Listen close, the stories breathe,
In every crevice, we must believe.
For beneath the bark, secrets lie,
Tales of earth, the truth, and why.

So wander forth, let nature's call,
Guide your heart, embrace it all.
In every step, let wonders pry,
For beneath the bark, secrets lie.

Aurora of the Woodland Spirits

A glimmer dawns, the forest wakes,
With gentle whispers, the silence breaks.
Auroras dance through leaves and light,
Spirits of the woods take flight.

In woven rays, their laughter sings,
Each flicker sparks, the joy it brings.
With playful hearts, they twirl and glide,
In every shadow, their magic hides.

The brook babbles, a merry tune,
As sunlight bathes the morning moon.
A vibrant glow, in hues of gold,
The woodland spirits, stories told.

Wander and wonder, journey far,
Follow the light of the brightest star.
For in this realm, the spirits roam,
In every heart, they find a home.

So cast away your doubts and fears,
Embrace the magic with joyful tears.
In the aurora, let your dreams collide,
With woodland spirits as your guide.

Sublime Twists of Fate in the Foliage

In tangled threads of emerald green,
Life unfolds, a vibrant scene.
Sublime twists of fate do sway,
Between the leaves, they find their way.

Each path diverges, yet entwines,
A dance of chance in whispered signs.
The sunbeams play, the shadows shift,
In nature's arms, the spirits drift.

With every rustle, a choice is made,
In the heart of the wood, no vow displayed.
Yet, still it feels like destiny,
Turning moments into memory.

The winds of change, they twist and bend,
Guiding us toward the journey's end.
Through every trial, the foliage gleams,
Showing us the way through dreams.

So dance among the rich array,
Where fate and fortune gently play.
In the sublime twists, we find our grace,
In nature's weave, we find our place.

Surreal Echoes in the Secret Glade

In twilight's breath, shadows dance,
Whispers of dreams in a fleeting trance.
Moonlight glimmers on silver leaves,
Secrets murmur where time conceives.

Painted skies in muted hues,
Beneath the boughs, the night muse snooze.
Echoes ripple through the air,
Lost in illusions, unaware.

Dew-kissed petals hold the night,
Fragrant memories take their flight.
A fleeting glimpse of forgotten lore,
Calling softly from ancient door.

The heartbeat of the verdant floor,
Cradling dreams forevermore.
With every sigh, the glade awakes,
In surreal tones, the essence breaks.

Time stands still, the world aglow,
In echoes soft, the secrets flow.
The nightingale sings a haunting tune,
Cradled under the watchful moon.

Tales from the Whispering Willows

In silence wraps the willow's weep,
Secrets buried shadows keep.
Stories linger on the breeze,
Softly spoken through the trees.

Branches sway with graceful sway,
Guiding whispers night and day.
A tapestry of age-old tales,
Woven gently where time prevails.

Beneath the curve of emerald leaves,
Dreams awaken, while the heart believes.
In misty breaths, old voices call,
To the world hidden, beyond the fall.

With every rustle, history glows,
Carrying stories only the wind knows.
Threads of fate entwined and spun,
In the shadows where tales run.

Laughter echoes, and sorrows blend,
In the haven where the branches bend.
Life's river flows without a care,
In tales whispered under the air.

Flickering Lights Beneath the Canopy

Stars descend in playful gleam,
Through tangled vines, they weave a dream.
Flickers dance on the forest floor,
Inviting souls to seek and explore.

Shadows hide in rhythmic sway,
Where the fireflies choose to play.
Nature's jewels, a brilliant embrace,
Casting light in this enchanted space.

The night unfolds with whispered sighs,
A million wonders in the sky.
Every flicker, a tale of night,
Binding hearts in soft twilight.

Moonlit paths beckon with grace,
Through the darkness, we find our place.
An ethereal glow, a gentle guide,
In this magical, wild ride.

Underneath the canopy vast,
Fleeting moments held fast.
With each flicker, a promise made,
In the light of the serenade.

Dreams Woven with Foliage and Starlight

In starlit realms where dreams do dwell,
Tangled hopes weave a silken spell.
Beneath the leaves, the magic glows,
In whispered winds, the dreamer knows.

Threads of silver, soft and bright,
Intertwined through the dark night.
Foliage cradles starry sighs,
In the embrace where freedom flies.

Crickets sing a lullaby sweet,
Guiding dreams on gentle feet.
In this haven where wishes bloom,
Shadows bloom in twilight's room.

Every leaf a storied page,
In forest depths, we find our stage.
With every breath, the night expands,
Holding dreams in tender hands.

From living tapestries, we are spun,
Dancing freely till night is done.
In the heart of the sleeping wood,
Dreams awaken, woven good.

The Language of Leaves Surrounded by Solitude

In whispering winds, the leaves confide,
Secrets of silence where shadows abide.
Gentle rustles echo soft pleas,
Nature's own tales stir deep in the trees.

Each fluttering note, a story unfolds,
Of seasons long gone, and memories bold.
Beneath the vast sky, where stillness reigns,
The language of leaves in sweet refrains.

Amidst quiet paths, where few ever tread,
Lies wisdom in whispers that nature has spread.
Alone with the spirit of earth's boundless grace,
The heart finds its rhythm, a tranquil embrace.

Solitude sings in the cool, crisp air,
With every leaf falling, a prayer laid bare.
In the golden glow, time seems to cease,
As shadows take root, and the soul finds peace.

The ground becomes music, each step a soft rhyme,
Threads woven gently through the fabric of time.
Listening close, the world comes alive,
In the language of leaves, the heart will thrive.

Echoing Secrets from the Heart of the Wild

In the depths of the forest, where secrets reside,
Echoes of whispers drift softly outside.
The wild holds its breath, cloaked in the night,
As shadows dance lightly in flickering light.

Crickets sing songs of the moon's gentle glow,
While winds tell of places that few may know.
In the heart of the wild, treasures untold,
Each secret a promise, a story to hold.

The rustling leaves weave a tapestry fine,
Of dreams mingling softly with whispers divine.
Ancient trees stand guard, with wisdom in bark,
Sheltering echoes that linger in dark.

Stars blink in the heavens, lending their gaze,
To the pulse of the wild, through a shimmering haze.
Nature breathes softly, a lullaby sweet,
As the heart of the wild finds its rhythmic beat.

Listen closely, and hear the delight,
Of secrets unfolding in the still of the night.
With every soft rustle and call from afar,
The echoes of nature are never too far.

Phantoms of Past in the Misty Glen

In the misty glen, where shadows convene,
Phantoms of past dance, elusive and keen.
They glide through the fog with a knowing embrace,
Whispers of history, time's gentle trace.

Each step on the path breathes stories so old,
Of laughter and tears, in memories bold.
Branches adorned with a silvery shroud,
Echo the tales of the lost and the proud.

The air is thick with the weight of their song,
A symphony haunting, where echoes belong.
With footsteps like whispers, they wander the night,
In search of the light, where shadows take flight.

A gentle resolve in the heart of the glen,
Where past meets the present, time swirls like a pen.
Misty tendrils curl, a soft, ghostly veil,
Reminders of journeys where few prevail.

In the stillness, a promise, a bond we can feel,
With phantoms of past, a story surreal.
The glen breathes life into echoes anew,
In the fog of remembrance, we find something true.

Capricious Colors on the Forest Floor

In the heart of the woods, where sunlight spills,
Capricious colors play on the hills.
Dappled hues shimmer, a vivid array,
Whispers of nature in bold, bright display.

Moss blankets stones, a soft emerald quilt,
While blooms burst with laughter, and silence is skilled.
Violet blooms peek from beneath leafy thrones,
In a world where the wild claims its vibrant tones.

Golden leaves tumble, in waltzes they twirl,
As the forest unfurls, like a painter's great swirl.
Crimson and amber ignite in delight,
While shadows grow long with the fading light.

Every step reveals a canvas adorned,
With stories born fresh in colors transformed.
Cascading the light, in patterns that flow,
A feast for the senses, the forest aglow.

Among this kaleidoscope, beauty and grace,
Nature enchants with its intricate lace.
In the heart of the forest, where colors collide,
Life's capricious palette offers dreams to abide.

Reflections in the Moss-Kissed Twilight

In twilight's hush, the secrets breathe,
Moss-kissed whispers weave beneath.
Shadows dance on ancient trees,
Carrying tales on the evening breeze.

The brook's soft song, a gentle pull,
Guides the heart where dreams are full.
Stars peek through a linen sky,
While the night wraps memories nigh.

A moment lingers, fleeting charm,
Nature sways with a tender calm.
Reflections glimmer on darkened streams,
For in this twilight, we find our dreams.

Glints of Luminous Dreams

In the quiet night, dreams take flight,
Glints of silver in soft moonlight.
Each thought dances like fireflies,
Beneath the canvas of starry skies.

Drifting softly on milky beams,
Whispers of hope ignite our dreams.
With every pulse, the heart does soar,
Unraveling tales of evermore.

A melody plays, sweet and clear,
Echoing visions we hold dear.
In these moments, we find our face,
In glints of dreams, we find our place.

Veils of Verdant Illusion

Among leaves green, an illusion grows,
Veils of verdant, where mystery flows.
Light filters down in spots of gold,
A story whispered, soft and bold.

Petals flutter in a gentle ballet,
Nature's canvas in bright array.
Hidden paths invite us near,
To wander deep without a fear.

In this realm, the senses dance,
Wrapped in nature's sweet romance.
Veils of illusion, woven tight,
Lead us onward through the night.

The Elfin Veil and the Moonlit Dance

Beneath the elfin veil so fine,
A dance unfolds, both bright and divine.
Moonlit beams trace every twirl,
As stars in awe begin to swirl.

Glimmers mingle in the night air,
Joining shadows in whispered prayer.
Laughter echoes through the glade,
Where magic blooms and fears fade.

With every step, the world retreats,
As enchantment wraps in gentle greets.
The night knows well this timeless chance,
In the elfin veil and moonlit dance.

The Pulse of Wandering Elves Beneath Stars

In glades where shadows softly play,
The elves do dance until the gray.
Their laughter sparkles through the night,
As stars above share secret light.

With whispers woven in the breeze,
They chase the dreams of ancient trees.
A twinkle here, a shimmer there,
They drift through worlds beyond compare.

Their footsteps kiss the dew-kissed grass,
In moments fleeting, hours pass.
The moonlit path, a silver thread,
Guides them where only few have tread.

Beneath the sky, in gentle trance,
They tell their tales, their fabled dance.
With every note, a heart will stir,
In echoes soft, the woods confer.

The night descends, but still they roam,
In nature's cradle, they find home.
With every star, a story spun,
In elven realms, the night is won.

Echoes of the Unseen in Leafy Embrace

In hidden nooks, the whispers gleam,
Where light and shadow softly dream.
The leaves embrace the stories told,
In every gust, a secret's gold.

The roots entwined in earthy bliss,
Know tales of life, of love, of kiss.
With every rustle, tales are shared,
Of moments lost, of hearts that dared.

Beneath the boughs, the spirits sigh,
As time unfolds, they watch and cry.
The echoes carry through the years,
A gentle balm for hidden fears.

The air is thick with memories bright,
As nature weaves her purest light.
In leafy embrace, solace sought,
Whispers of the unseen are caught.

In harmony, the forest sways,
As life renews in countless ways.
Each heartbeat echoes through the trees,
In timeless dance, the spirit frees.

Tales Sown Deep in Rooted Reverie

Within the soil, the stories lie,
Of time long past and days gone by.
The roots entwine, a timeless thread,
In every grain, the dreams are fed.

Beneath the surface, whispers dwell,
Of ancient trees and fragrant swell.
They keep the secrets of the land,
In silent watch, they understand.

The dance of seasons, sharp and sweet,
With tender rains, the earth's heartbeat.
In every sprout, a hope takes flight,
As nature writes her pure delight.

In reverie, the past invokes,
A tapestry of nature's yokes.
The stories sown in every seam,
Are woven strong, they pulse and beam.

Through tender roots, the tales are cast,
In lingering echoes from the past.
Embrace the essence of the green,
For in these whispers, life is seen.

The Subtle Art of Nature's Whimsy

In shimmering dawn, a bird takes flight,
With wings like laughter, pure delight.
The sun peeks through with golden rays,
A gentle start to tranquil days.

The brook sings sweetly, clear and bright,
A melody of soft invite.
With every ripple, life anew,
The art of nature, tried and true.

The flowers nod in playful glee,
As petals sway, so free, so free.
With colors bold and scents unique,
Each bloom a story, gently speak.

The whispering wind, a soft caress,
Unfolds the magic, nothing less.
In every gust, her secrets sway,
Nature's whimsy at play, hooray!

As twilight beckons, stars ignite,
The world transforms in soft twilight.
In nature's arms, all fears subside,
The subtle art of joy and pride.

Secrets Danced in the Dappled Glimpse

In a quiet glade where shadows play,
Whispers of dreams in the soft light sway.
Leaves above murmur secrets untold,
Fragrant blooms in colors bold.

Moonbeams twinkle through branches fine,
Casting a glow on the paths that intertwine.
Footsteps soft on the carpet of green,
Nature's beauty, a wonder unseen.

Laughter echoes in the breeze's song,
As twilight falls and the night grows long.
Stars peek down, their stories alive,
In the heart of the forest, mysteries thrive.

A flicker here, a flutter there,
Magic dances in the cool night air.
Each shadow holds a tale to share,
In this dappled glimpse, we wander rare.

So linger long where the secrets sigh,
And let your imagination soar high.
For in this place of serene delight,
The soul finds peace in the quiet night.

The Lurking Magic of Hidden Woods

Deep in the woods where the old trees stand,
A realm untouched by human hand.
Spellbinding whispers drift on the breeze,
And ancient magic dwells with ease.

Crimson flowers bloom with a knowing grin,
Guarding the secrets hidden within.
The brook babbles softly, a tale of its own,
Of creatures and spirits in realms unknown.

Fog blankets the ground like a gentle sigh,
As shadows stretch out and the owls reply.
With every rustle and every sound,
Mysteries hidden, a world profound.

A path weaves onward, mysterious and wild,
Inviting the heart of both sage and child.
In the heart of the wood, enchantments await,
With memories forged that time cannot sate.

So tread lightly, dear friend, through this sacred land,
With eyes that can see and a heart that can stand.
For the lurking magic, it's waiting for thee,
In the hidden woods, where you might be free.

Fables Twisted with Nature's Ink

In the whispering trees, fables intertwine,
Each leaf tells a story, both yours and mine.
Nature's ink flows in the breeze so sweet,
With tales of the earth beneath our feet.

A fox in the dusk, a wise owl at dawn,
Partake in their wisdom as we carry on.
The brook sings of creatures, wrapped in its dream,
As we wander through stories that breathe and beam.

From mountains to valleys, in shadows they cling,
Stories of seasons, of winter and spring.
With every soft rustle and dance of the grass,
Fables unfold as the moments pass.

The twist of a tale lingers on the air,
In the heart of the forest, in the beauty laid bare.
With nature as scribe, the ink flows deep,
As we gather the stories for us to keep.

So listen intently to the winds that sigh,
And let nature's fables teach you to fly.
For in every corner where wild things roam,
Lives the spirit of fables, calling you home.

Celestial Glimpses Through Twisted Boughs

Amid tangled branches, where shadows lie,
Starry dreams flicker in the night sky.
With each gentle rustle of leaf and vine,
Celestial glimpses in beauty align.

Moonlight drips down through the branches so tight,
Illuminating paths in the cool, quiet night.
A dance of the cosmos, a spark in the dark,
Awakening wonders with each subtle spark.

The owls sing songs that echo the stars,
As magic weaves softly from Venus to Mars.
Each twinkling light tells a story anew,
In the embrace of the night, the world feels true.

Through twisted boughs, glimpses of grace,
With whispers of galaxies, we find our place.
Hearts uplifted by the beauty we see,
In the endless expanse of night's tapestry.

So wander beneath the celestial dome,
With each step you take, feel the universe roam.
For within the embrace of the night's gentle balm,
Lie celestial glimpses, an infinite calm.

Kaleidoscope Dreams Under the Ancient Boughs

Beneath the ancient boughs we lay,
Colors swirl in vivid array.
Dreams like whispers dance and weave,
In twilight's glow, we dare to believe.

Shadows drape the ground like lace,
Each pattern reveals a hidden place.
Moonlight spills through leaves that sigh,
While secrets twinkle in the sky.

Time unfolds its gentle hand,
As we lose track in this wonderland.
Every breath a symphony,
In this realm of possibility.

Stars adorn the velvet night,
Guiding us with ethereal light.
We are threads in a tapestry grand,
Woven together by fate's own hand.

So let us linger, hearts aligned,
In kaleidoscope dreams, love defined.
Under ancient boughs we find our truth,
In the soft embrace of eternal youth.

Nature's Veil: A Tapestry of Secrets

Within the woods, a secret's spun,
Nature whispers, her work begun.
Veils of green hide stories old,
Each leaf a tale quietly told.

Rivers weave through emerald seams,
Carrying the hush of dreams.
Branches bend with age's grace,
Guardians of this sacred place.

Mossy stones and twilight's hue,
Frame the path where shadows grew.
Footsteps echo, soft yet clear,
As if the earth holds us dear.

Wildflowers bloom, a patchwork bright,
Dancing softly in golden light.
In this embrace of gentle shade,
Life's rich tapestry is laid.

We wander deeper, hearts unveiled,
In nature's breath, we are inhaled.
Secrets woven, a soft caress,
In nature's veil, we find our rest.

Enchantment Lurks in the Glistening Leaves

A shimmering dew adorns the morn,
Each leaf a gem, a new life born.
Sunshine spills through canopies bright,
Awakening magic in golden light.

Whispers of nature, soft and sweet,
Guide our feet down the winding street.
With every rustle, a story will tell,
Of wonders hidden, where enchantments dwell.

Boughs sway gently, in soft embrace,
Inviting us into this vibrant space.
The air is thick with mysteries grand,
In the breathing woods, we understand.

Songs of the forest in harmony play,
Pulling us close, we're drawn to stay.
In emerald shadows, we chase the sun,
As the day unfolds, our spirits run.

So linger here where enchantments thrive,
In glistening leaves, we feel alive.
With every heartbeat, wonders renew,
In nature's embrace, dreams come true.

Chasing Whispers in Sylvan Glades

In sylvan glades where shadows prance,
We chase the whispers, lost in a trance.
Soft laughter rides the gentle breeze,
As we wander 'neath the towering trees.

Footfalls lightly grace the earth,
Where secrets bloom, and dreams give birth.
Every rustling leaf a call to explore,
In the heart of the woods, we crave more.

Patches of sunlight warm our face,
Each moment held in nature's embrace.
Through the thickets, we roam and gleam,
In sylvan glades, we live the dream.

Time flows softly, like a river's song,
In this enchanted realm, we belong.
With hearts aglow and spirits free,
Chasing whispers, just you and me.

As twilight falls, the world is hushed,
In fading light, our worries crushed.
Together we dance, with the stars above,
Chasing whispers, in nature's love.

Luminous Footprints in the Twilight

In the stillness of dusk's embrace,
Shadows blend with a warm trace.
Footprints glow on the path so bright,
Guiding souls through the falling night.

Whispers dance in the evening air,
Secrets shared, a tender care.
Stars awaken, one by one,
To cradle dreams till night is done.

The moon spills silver on the ground,
A symphony with a gentle sound.
All around, the world takes flight,
In luminous footprints of the night.

Echoes linger with every breath,
Life's soft chorus defying death.
In twilight's hold, we weave and wend,
Toward horizons where journeys blend.

So step boldly into the glow,
Let your heart and spirit flow.
For in this realm of fading light,
Luminous footprints lead us right.

Dappled Sunlight and Echoing Laughter

Through the leaves, the sunlight plays,
Casting patterns in warm arrays.
Children run with joy and cheer,
Echoes of laughter, bright and clear.

Nature's canvas springs to life,
Hearts are free, devoid of strife.
Moments melt like sweet ice cream,
In dappled sunlight, hearts do beam.

Bees hum low in the fragrant air,
While blossoms dance without a care.
All around, the world delights,
With whispers soft from day to nights.

Picnic blankets spread with ease,
Underneath the swaying trees.
Stories blend, laughter intertwines,
In every heart, the joy of shines.

For in this moment, time stands still,
Dappled sunlight, a gentle thrill.
Let echo laughter call your name,
As we embrace this vibrant game.

The Elusive Dance of Forest Lore

In the heart of emerald trees,
Mysteries sway with every breeze.
Whispered tales of ages past,
In the forest, shadows cast.

Elusive dance of sprite and deer,
Nature's magic whispers near.
As sunlight breaks through leaves so high,
A hidden world beneath the sky.

Ancient roots twist and intertwine,
Guard the secrets like aged wine.
Footsteps echo on the lichen floor,
The forest breathes its ancient lore.

Dappled light on a hidden glade,
Where fables old have softly played.
In every rustle, there's a song,
Calling us to the wild, belong.

So listen close to the woods' refrain,
In the stillness, joy and pain.
The elusive dance of forest lore,
Awakens hearts forevermore.

Tints of Magic in Nature's Breath

Morning dew, a soft caress,
Nature wakes in sweet finesse.
Colors bloom where petals grow,
Tints of magic in every flow.

Crimson, violet, and deep gold,
Stories in each hue retold.
In each blink, the world astounds,
As beauty whispers all around.

Rivers sing a liquid tune,
Reflecting the whispers of the moon.
Mountains cradle clouds so white,
Tints of magic wrap the night.

Each whisper of the winds that sway,
Sings of wonders in bright array.
With every step, the heart is free,
Nature's breath, a symphony.

So pause a while, let wonders greet,
Feel the magic, soft and sweet.
In nature's colors, find your quest,
For in her arms, we are truly blessed.

Threads of Enchantment Between the Trees

In the forest deep and wide,
Whispers dance with gentle pride.
Moonbeams weave through leaves so green,
Promises of magic, rarely seen.

Crickets sing a twilight tune,
Stars awaken, one by one.
Shadows play with fleeting light,
A world transformed by the night.

Branches stretch with open arms,
Embracing all their hidden charms.
Nature's secrets softly sway,
In this enchanted, wild ballet.

Morning dew on petals glistens,
Each drop holds the dreams we miss.
A tapestry of life unfolds,
In every thread, a story told.

Beneath the boughs, where silence breathes,
The heart finds peace amidst the leaves.
With every step, adventure calls,
In this grove where magic sprawls.

Flickering Lights in a Shaded World

Underneath the canopy,
A flicker bursts, a sight to see.
Fireflies dance in evening's glow,
Chasing dreams where shadows flow.

Murmurs blend with rustling leaves,
Carried on the night's soft breeze.
In this realm where darkness hums,
The heart hears secrets, softly drums.

Colors shift as night descends,
Each moment holds, as daylight ends.
Softly glowing, time drifts away,
In the dim, where wonders play.

Beneath the stars, the world feels small,
Yet within, it holds it all.
Mysteries woven in light and shade,
In twilight's arms, our fears are laid.

A gentle hush calls to my soul,
In the dark, I feel whole.
Dancing lights, a fleeting spark,
Guide my heart through the dark.

Whirlwinds of Color in the Maple's Arms

In the heart of autumn's kiss,
Whirls of color draw us to bliss.
Crimson leaves beneath our feet,
Nature's carpet, warm and sweet.

Branches sway in gentle dance,
As breezes play, they take their chance.
Gold and rust in the bright sun,
A symphony that can't be undone.

Each twirl reveals a hidden muse,
In every shade, a world to choose.
Whispers of the past reside,
Among the trees where dreams abide.

Beneath the boughs, we close our eyes,
Floating with the winds that rise.
Time stands still, the moment swells,
In the magic that nature tells.

As the daylight starts to fade,
In each swirl, memories made.
A canvas painted by the breeze,
A story shared among the trees.

Glints of Wonder in Humble Hollows

In secluded nooks where shadows lie,
Glints of wonder catch the eye.
Fragments of light on mossy green,
Nature's gems, simple yet keen.

From rocky crevices, life will peek,
In silent whispers, it starts to speak.
Tiny blooms in colors bright,
Glisten softly in fading light.

Humble hollows cradle dreams,
Where each moment, magic seems.
A world away, yet close at hand,
In this untouched, sacred land.

Echoes of laughter, soft and clear,
In these depths, we shed our fear.
Lessons learned from earth and stone,
In nature's heart, we find our own.

So let us wander where few have trod,
In the hollows, feel the nod.
With every glimmer, hope takes flight,
In the simplest, pure delight.

The Veiled Symphony of Sylvan Spirits

Whispers dance through ancient trees,
A melody of rustling leaves.
Shadows play in dappled light,
Sylvan spirits take their flight.

Fingers trace the bark's embrace,
Secrets held in nature's grace.
Notes of laughter in the air,
Echoes of a world so rare.

Moonlit paths where shadows sway,
Guide the lost, show them the way.
With each step, their hearts will soar,
To the heart of the forest floor.

In the quiet, a song so true,
Springs of life in every hue.
Veiled in mist, the spirits hum,
A symphony, they softly drum.

Find your peace among the trees,
Join the chorus of the breeze.
The veiled symphony unfolds,
Stories of the forest told.

Mirage of Dreams in the Weaving Woods

In the weaving woods, dreams explore,
A mirage dances on the floor.
Colors blend and shadows play,
Guiding wanderers on their way.

Whispers float on gentle streams,
Carrying the heart's soft dreams.
Branches arch like lovers' arms,
Holding secrets, nature's charms.

Footsteps trace the paths of old,
Tales of magic yet untold.
Misty visions, foggy sights,
Guide the dreamers through the nights.

Every turn unveils a chance,
To lose oneself in forest dance.
Leaves of amber, gold, and green,
Paint the canvas, serene, unseen.

The mirage of dreams persists,
In the woods where hope exists.
A call to those who dare to see,
The wonders of what can be.

Eclipsed Lights Beyond the Hollowed Logs

In shadows cast by hollowed logs,
Eclipsed lights twinkle like frogs.
Hidden gems in twilight's fold,
Stories whisper, softly told.

Glimmers dance in twilight's hue,
Secrets shared, just me and you.
Fainting stars in a midnight sky,
Echoes of the night's soft sigh.

Wandering hearts find their way,
Cradled by the night's ballet.
Moonlit paths of silver dreams,
Illuminate the forest seams.

Past the logs where shadows creep,
Mysteries of the woods do keep.
Eclipsed lights, in silence hum,
Inviting hearts to feel the drum.

Through the night where spirits glow,
In the dark, let wonder flow.
Eclipsed lights, a guiding spark,
Lead the seekers through the dark.

Colorful Anecdotes of the Glistening Trail

On the glistening trail, colors sing,
Nature's palette, a thriving spring.
Blooming tales in every shade,
Whispers of joy, none can fade.

Petals dance in the morning light,
Colorful specimens, pure delight.
Butterflies frolic, gentle flight,
Painting dreams in vibrant sight.

Each turn brings a brand-new tale,
Echoes of laughter on the trail.
Fruits of life in radiant hues,
Anecdotes shared, old and new.

Beneath the arches of the trees,
Sway the branches in the breeze.
Nature's stories, softly told,
In the glistening trail of gold.

Colorful anecdotes arise,
Under the vast and boundless skies.
Step by step, let wonder prevail,
Join the dance on the glistening trail.

Whims of the Glimmering Glade

In the glade where whispers play,
Light dances, night meets day.
Petals shimmer, dew drops cling,
Softly woven, the dreams they bring.

Colors burst, a vibrant hue,
Underneath the skies so blue.
Nature's song begins to swell,
Telling tales the woods could tell.

Breezes weave through ancient trees,
Carrying secrets on the breeze.
Mossy carpets, lush and wide,
Hold the stories deep inside.

Glimmering sparks in twilight's glow,
Invite the heart to ebb and flow.
In every shadow, a chance to find,
The wonders of a world unlined.

Whims of magic bid us stay,
In the glade where dreams hold sway.
Step lightly through the tranquil scene,
Where glimmer meets serene.

The Allure of Hidden Pathways

Amidst the thickets, trails unfold,
Stories of the wild are told.
Twisting routes, both sharp and smooth,
Draw the wanderers who seek to soothe.

Leaves whisper softly in the air,
Secrets linger everywhere.
Where do these winding paths lead?
A place for hearts that dare to heed.

Sunlight filters through the green,
Crafting shadows, pure and clean.
Each footstep echoes, soft and light,
Illuminating dreams in flight.

Beneath the boughs, adventures call,
Inviting those who fear to fall.
Hidden pathways, wild and free,
Guide the restless, lead to glee.

In the depths of whispering woods,
Life unfolds in gentle moods.
The allure of trails yet unseen,
Awakens all the hearts that dream.

Dreamlike Shades Beneath Enchanted Canopies

From lofty heights, the branches sigh,
Whispers of myths drift gently by.
In twilight's cloak, the shadows play,
Dreamlike shades dance night and day.

Beneath the canopy, still and vast,
Memories linger of the past.
Embraced by shadows, soft and slight,
A realm where dreams take wing in flight.

Murmurs of magic, sweet and rare,
Wind through the leaves, hang in the air.
Each glimmering ray, a fleeting wish,
Nurtured gently like a silken kiss.

Wandering hearts find solace here,
In shaded realms where hope is clear.
Beneath the boughs, where visions stream,
We join the dance of every dream.

In the stillness, secrets unfold,
Of enchanted tales yet untold.
Forever, we seek the bliss we crave,
In dreamlike shades that nature gave.

Radiant Murmurs of the Breathing Earth

Upon the crest of rolling hills,
The earth awakens, and time stills.
Radiant murmurs weave through grass,
Nature's heartbeat, soft and vast.

With every step, a song is sung,
By creatures old and spirits young.
The mountains whisper, rivers glide,
In every pulse, the soul does bide.

Crimson sunsets, vibrant skies,
Invite the heart, where stillness lies.
Beneath the stars, the night unfurls,
A cosmic dance of distant worlds.

Feet upon the earthy floor,
We listen, listen, seek for more.
Every shadow, every beam,
Carves the space for hopes to dream.

The radiant whispers, strong and clear,
Echo the truth that all can hear.
In the solitude of nature's mirth,
We find the joy of breathing earth.

The Elusion of Magic in the Tanglewood

In Tanglewood where whispers play,
The trees hold secrets, night and day.
Beneath the boughs, the shadows dance,
A fleeting glimpse of fate's romance.

The light fades gently into dusk,
Among the leaves, a soft, sweet musk.
A hidden realm where dreams reside,
In nature's arms, our hearts confide.

An echo's laughter haunts the glade,
Where ancient tales of magic fade.
With every step, the ground will thrum,
A beating heart, to which we come.

Through tangled vines, a pathway bends,
Where time itself seems to suspend.
The air is thick with spellbound air,
An invitation, rare and fair.

Yet as we search for fleeting light,
The magic hides just out of sight.
In Tanglewood, the dreams may weave,
An endless tale for those who believe.

Shadows of Enchantment Writ in Dappled Light

In dappled light, the shadows play,
A world of wonder, bright as day.
Through emerald leaves, a soft glow beams,
As nature spins her ancient dreams.

The sun descends behind the trees,
While whispers ride on gentle breeze.
Each rustle weaves a story old,
In every spark, a memory told.

Amid the glade, the fairies twirl,
As secrets from the forest swirl.
Their laughter sings in muted tones,
In harmony with ancient bones.

A waltz of shadows, light entwined,
Where ethereal paths are designed.
Bewitched by wonders yet unseen,
We roam our hearts in blissful sheen.

Yet as the evening starts to wane,
The fleeting beauty cloaks in rain.
Yet in our hearts, the magic stays,
A lingering taste of sunlit days.

Secrets Entwined in Nature's Embrace

In nature's arms, we find our way,
Where secrets hide in bright array.
Among the ferns, the silence breathes,
With every rustle, truth believes.

The mossy stones hold tales untold,
Of lives once lived, both brave and bold.
Each fallen leaf, a whispered note,
In symphonies that shadows wrote.

The brook sings softly, lullabies sweet,
In gentle rhythm, hearts will meet.
As sunbeam kisses, dew will rise,
With every dawn, our spirits fly.

Beneath the boughs, the time suspends,
As nature's beauty never ends.
In every glance, a world unfolds,
A magic found, a love that holds.

Yet often lost, we stray away,
From nature's path in disarray.
But when we pause, and breathe the air,
We find our peace, we find our care.

Enigmatic Patterns of the Woodland Weave

In woodland realms, the patterns glow,
A tapestry that ebbs and flows.
Each thread a tale of life and death,
The whispers linger, holding breath.

Amid the trees, a rhythm beats,
Where every shadow, mystery greets.
With footprints left, we walk the line,
Between the past and what's divine.

In tangled roots, the stories twist,
Of creatures lost in twilight mist.
Their echoes haunt the silent air,
A secret weave of hope and care.

The moonlight bathes the branches wide,
With silver threads of dreams inside.
In patterns woven, fate aligns,
As night bequeaths its quiet signs.

Yet in the morning's light, we wake,
To find the magic we must take.
With open hearts, we'll dare to see,
The enigmatic tapestry.

Whispers of Color in the Forest Shade

In the stillness where shadows play,
Colors dance in the light of day.
Leaves shimmer in a gentle breeze,
Whispers linger among the trees.

Sunlight filters through emerald strains,
Painting patterns like soft refrains.
Each hue tells a story untold,
In nature's embrace, we find the gold.

Violet blooms in a hidden nook,
Crimson berries in a babbling brook.
In this realm where silence sings,
Nature's canvas, it offers wings.

Golden rays catch the dew-kissed grass,
Moments linger, too sweet to pass.
A symphony of color so bright,
Whispers of wonder in forest light.

In twilight's hush, shadows extend,
A tapestry woven where colors blend.
Beneath the boughs, we find our place,
In whispers of color, we find our grace.

Enigmatic Glimmers Beneath the Canopy

Beneath the canopy, secrets hide,
Enigmatic glimmers, shadows glide.
Dappled light spills, a fleeting glance,
Where ferns sway in a timeless dance.

Echoes whisper through the tall trees,
Stories carried on the soft breeze.
Moss carpets the earth, lush and green,
A hidden world, so barely seen.

Intriguing shapes in twilight's haze,
Where mysteries weave in nature's maze.
Glimmers of hope in the quiet night,
A flicker of dreams in fading light.

With every rustle, a tale unfolds,
Of ancient paths and whispers bold.
Each step taken, a journey begun,
In this enchanting realm, we run.

Stars peek through the emerald veil,
Guiding us softly on the trail.
Beneath the canopy, hearts entwine,
In their embrace, we feel divine.

Secrets Woven in Twilight's Threads

Twilight descends with its gentle weave,
Secrets whispered to those who believe.
Threads of light stitch the fabric of night,
A tapestry shimmering, soft and slight.

Each shadow is painted with care,
Stories resting on the cool air.
Moonlight drapes over the sleeping ground,
In hushed tones, the world spins around.

Stars twinkle in a darkened sky,
Guarding the dreams as they softly fly.
Woven softly in the dusk's embrace,
Twilight gathers the night's warm face.

Nature sighs, ready to sleep,
Cradling secrets it vows to keep.
With every rustle, a promise made,
In twilight's glow, our fears do fade.

The forest holds what words cannot say,
In sacred silence, we drift away.
Secrets woven in twilight's threads,
Speak softly as the daylight sheds.

Elven Shadows and Faded Echoes

In twilight's glow, the Elven shadows sway,
Ancient whispers in the woods convey.
Faded echoes of songs long past,
Dance through branches, their grip holds fast.

Moonlit paths weave in the night air,
Every step taken with gentle care.
Mysteries linger where the starlight falls,
Wrapped in silence, the forest calls.

Time stands still in this sacred space,
Embraced by magic, we find our place.
Elven laughter rides on the wind,
A reminder of the joys we send.

Underneath the canopy's dark shield,
Hidden truths are quietly revealed.
Softly we wander as spirits unite,
In the depths of the enchanted night.

Here in the twilight, we sigh and dream,
Elven shadows play with the moonbeam.
As echoes fade into the soft glow,
Our hearts remember what we long to know.

Hidden Reflections on Mossy Stones

Beneath the moss, secrets lie,
Whispers of water, soft and sly.
A mirror of green, in soft light shown,
Nature's embrace, where dreams are grown.

The stones, they cradle, time and fate,
In their stillness, memories wait.
Each ripple dances, a fleeting glance,
In the quiet, the heart finds its chance.

Sunlight dapples, a gentle kiss,
On the surface, the world feels bliss.
Reflected stories of days gone by,
Under the canopy, the softest sigh.

In shadows deep, a tale unfolds,
Of ages past, as silent as folds.
Mossy guardians, they stand in peace,
Holding the moments, our minds release.

Hidden reflections, nature's art,
Call to the wanderer, to seek his heart.
Among the stones, life's wisdom grows,
In this sanctuary, the spirit knows.

The Lure of the Enchanted Grove

In twilight's glow, the woodlands sigh,
A whispering breeze, a soft goodbye.
The path diverges, a secret way,
Calling the hearts that wish to stay.

Ancient trees in emerald hue,
Veil mysteries old, and tales anew.
Their branches cradle, the moonlit beam,
As starlit echoes weave a dream.

Magic stirs in the underbrush,
The fireflies flicker, a gentle hush.
Crickets serenade the night so clear,
While shadows dance, bringing near.

With every step, the air grows sweet,
The luring scent of earth and heat.
Lost in this grove of the fantasy,
The heart beats wild, the spirit flies free.

Beneath the canopy, souls intertwine,
In the enchanted's arms, the heart will dine.
A promise lingers, forever bold,
In the grove's embrace, we are consoled.

Shades of Magic in the Quiet Woods

In the quiet woods, where whispers bloom,
Shadows entwine in the cool, dim gloom.
Glimmers of light through the branches peek,
Murmurs of magic, soft yet unique.

The air is thick with an ancient charm,
As nature wraps in a soothing arm.
Every rustle holds a secret untold,
As dreams unspool in the green and gold.

Petals unfurl like pages of lore,
Each step reveals so much more.
A chorus of leaves, a sonorous song,
Where every soul feels they belong.

Sunbeams scatter on the forest floor,
Creating paths to the mystical door.
In this sanctuary, the heart finds peace,
In the shades of magic, worries cease.

The quiet woods breathe stories deep,
In the silence, the ancients keep.
Each moment feels like a timeless gift,
Awash in shadows, souls will drift.

Stories Imprinted on Nature's Canvas

On nature's canvas, a tale unfolds,
In vibrant colors and strokes bold.
Each petal painted with the sun's delight,
In the afternoon glow, so warm, so bright.

Mountains rise like stories of old,
Guardians of wisdom, fierce and bold.
Rivers run deep with songs of the earth,
Each flow a reminder of life's great worth.

The sky becomes a tapestry vast,
Where clouds weave dreams of the present and past.
Birds trace paths in arcs of grace,
In nature's embrace, we find our place.

Whispers of winds sketch timeless lore,
As echoes linger along the shore.
Leaves drift softly like pages torn,
From books long lost, yet never worn.

Each moment reflects a brilliant hue,
In this grand gallery, life feels true.
Nature's stories, forever refined,
Imprinted in hearts, eternally entwined.

The Enchanted Lattice Above

Underneath the twinkling stars,
Whispers dance in night's embrace.
A lattice woven with dreams,
Holds secrets of a timeless place.

Moonlight spills on silver leaves,
Caressing whispers of the night.
A gentle breeze, soft and kind,
Invites the heart to take flight.

In shadows formed by ancient vines,
The tales of old begin to weave.
Each thread a story softly spins,
In the tapestry we believe.

Glimmers fade as dawn draws near,
Yet memories will never die.
In the quiet, they remain,
Beneath the vast, eternal sky.

Hold close the magic in your heart,
Let it guide your every move.
The lattice spun with starlit dreams,
Forever invites us to prove.

Dreams Adrift in the Pastel Mist

Hazy thoughts in morning glow,
Pastel shades of whispered dreams.
Winds of change gently blow,
Stirring life in slumber's seams.

Clouds of pink and softest blue,
Float like wishes in the air.
Each moment feels fresh and new,
Inviting all to dare and care.

Softly spoken, hopes take flight,
Carried by the dawn's first light.
In the mist, a dance unfolds,
Stories waiting to be told.

Wander through this waking haze,
With open heart and eyes aglow.
The world awakens in a daze,
Where true adventures start to grow.

Embrace the mystery within,
Let it guide you, free and bold.
In dreams adrift, let life begin,
A canvas bright, a tale retold.

Flutters of the Unseen Path

In twilight's hush, a whisper stirs,
Soft flutters brush against the breeze.
Paths unseen await the bold,
Filled with mysteries and leaves.

Footsteps light on dewy grass,
Echoes linger in the night.
Nature's call, a secret guide,
Leads the weary soul to light.

With every bend, a chance to see,
What lies beyond the fears we claim.
In flutters soft, we find our way,
Toward the heart of longing flame.

Through the darkness, courage grows,
With every step, a tale begins.
The unseen path, where greatness glows,
Beckons us to break our sins.

So journey forth, embrace the night,
With open arms and fearless heart.
For in these flutters, pure delight,
Awaits the brave who dare to start.

Shadows that Recall Forgotten Lores

In corners dim, where shadows play,
Echoes linger of days long past.
Stories whispered, time's soft sway,
In ancient halls where memories cast.

Dusty tomes, with secrets sealed,
Hold the weight of wisdom's grace.
Each page a glimpse, a truth revealed,
Tracing footsteps, a timeless chase.

Flickering candles, soft and low,
Illuminate the tales we've lost.
In voices hushed, the ages flow,
Reminding us of the heavy cost.

To hold the past in heart and mind,
Is to cherish all we've known.
Shadows dance, and we will find,
In their embrace, we are not alone.

So listen close, let shadows teach,
Recall the lores of days gone by.
In their arms, a gift they preach,
A guiding light that will not die.

Enigmatic Whispers of the Sylvan Realm

Beneath the canopy, secrets dwell,
Each rustling leaf, a story to tell.
The brook hums softly, its ancient tune,
In twilight's grasp, beneath the moon.

Shadows dance where the ferns unfold,
Mysteries beckon, both timid and bold.
The aroma of earth, wet and sweet,
Guides the curious, with nimble feet.

Elders stand guard with their gnarled arms,
Whispering legends of nature's charms.
A sigh of the winds, a flicker of light,
Embraces the wanderer, cloaked in night.

Through pathways lined with the softest green,
Every corner hides what's rarely seen.
An echoing call from a creature shy,
Lures the heart to wander and fly.

With every step, the spirits ignite,
An enchanting dance, an ethereal sight.
In this sylvan realm, where wonders play,
The enigmas of life guide the way.

Sorrows Shrouded in Leafy Lullabies

In the stillness, leaves start to weep,
A melody low, where shadows creep.
The wind carries tales, so soft and frail,
Of hearts once bright, now ghostly pale.

Branches cradle what once was whole,
Whispers of sorrows entwined in the soul.
A funeral hush blankets the ground,
In this leafy haven, lost dreams are found.

Crimson and gold fall, a slow goodbye,
As time unveils where memories lie.
The roots embrace what we've long let go,
In nature's arms, comfort flows slow.

Rustling voices speak of their pain,
In each sigh of the breeze, solace remains.
The dance of the shadows, a haunting refrain,
Echoes of joy wrapped in sorrow's chain.

Yet in the dark, a flicker of light,
Reminds us of hope, against the night.
For amidst the leaves, lullabies rhyme,
Telling us gently, we'll heal in time.

Elixirs of Twilight's Breath

The dusk descends with a tender sigh,
Colors swirl as day waves goodbye.
Golden hues mix with purples and gray,
Creating potions, at end of day.

Soft whispers of dusk drink in the sky,
Brews of enchantment, where dreams lie.
From blossom to bough, the flavors blend,
A tapestry woven where colors mend.

Each moment's a sip, sweet and divine,
The elixirs of twilight imbue as they twine.
With every blink, the stars begin to wink,
Inviting the heart to pause and think.

Clouds loom softly, like spirits in flight,
Stretching their arms through the fabric of night.
Nature's own whispers caress the earth,
Stirring the magic, igniting rebirth.

Within twilight's breath, we hold our dreams,
A communion with shadows, in soft moonbeams.
For in this hour, the world feels blessed,
Elixirs of night put our souls to rest.

Lanterns of Luminous Laughter

Beneath the starlit celestial dome,
Laughter cascades, a call to roam.
In meadows alive, where wildflowers sway,
Lanterns of joy dance through the fray.

Their glow ignites every heart's delight,
As shadows retreat and spirit takes flight.
Each chuckle, each giggle, a flickering spark,
Illuminates corners once hidden and dark.

The breeze carries whispers, buoyant and free,
Of tales intertwined with hugs and glee.
In the air, a sweetness hangs low,
As lanterns of laughter begin to glow.

Friendship blooms where the wild grass grows,
In the laughter shared, a bond beautifully shows.
With twinkling eyes, we dance in a ring,
Under soft moonlight, a joy-filled spring.

Every echo of joy, a story retold,
In the warmth of the night, the universe unfolds.
For amidst the joy, hearts find their way,
Lanterns of laughter guide us to stay.

Delicate Narratives in the Forest's Breath

In the hush of dawn's light, soft tales arise,
Whispers of leaves dance, under stretched skies.
Mossy carpets cushion each nimble foot,
While shadows weave secrets, in silent pursuit.

Sunbeams pierce gently, where stories unfold,
Each stem and each branch, a mystery told.
Echoes of whispers, where wild creatures dwell,
Cloaked in the fragrance of nature's sweet spell.

Rippling streams murmur, brush glistening stones,
Life blooms in the quiet, where beauty is sown.
Through thickets and groves, old narratives weave,
Inviting us closer, in heart to believe.

With each fleeting moment, the forest will sigh,
In delicate cadence, beneath the vast sky.
Time's gentle hand sketches the softest of dreams,
Enraptured by silence, where life softly gleams.

In whispers of breezes, the stories make way,
Every rustling leaf speaks of night and of day.
As twilight descends, the air turns to gold,
A symphony plays, in the breaths we behold.

Fading Legends in the Emerald Hush

Beneath the tall canopies, shadows confide,
Fables of yore in the emerald hide.
Each rustle and rustle, a fragment of old,
In soft, gentle murmurs, the legends are told.

Buried in brambles, where whispers collect,
Tales of the ancients find bright paths to reflect.
With every small flutter, the past lingers near,
As nature sings softly, a trance to revere.

The moss-covered stones hold the wisdom of years,
In delicate sighs, through laughter and tears.
Mirrored in stillness, where light gently glows,
Fading legends dance in the twilight's soft throes.

Crickets serenade, as the night drapes her shawl,
Echos embrace every heart-stirring call.
Whispers in shadows stretch long through the night,
In echoes of legend, life's stories ignite.

A soft symphony plays, under stars shining through,
The forest holds close the tales that ring true.
With each heartbeat echoing in soft emerald hush,
We weave with the legends that time cannot crush.

Twilight's Palette in the Whispering Grove

As daylight retreats, the colors take flight,
Twilight paints softly, the canvas of night.
With strokes of deep lavender, shadows grow tall,
In the whispers of trees, we hear nature's call.

The breeze carries secrets of dusk and of dawn,
A symphony woven until all light's gone.
Through the boughs of the grove, glimmers twinkle bright,
In twilight's embrace, hearts lift to new height.

Glowing soft fireflies, like stars drawn to play,
Dance through the branches, chasing worries away.
With each gentle flutter, colors blend true,
In the palette of twilight, we find something new.

Each leaf in the breeze sings songs of delight,
As whispers of dusky soft dreams take flight.
In the heart of the grove, every moment is sweet,
A tapestry woven where night and day meet.

The cool air embraces, invites us to linger,
While moonlight dips low, beckoning a finger.
To sketch in the twilight, a vision to keep,
In the whispers of shadows, we gently fall asleep.

Forgotten Footfalls on the Lush Trail

Along the lush trail, where wildflowers sway,
Footfalls of wanderers have passed on the way.
Vines drape in silence, as stories unwind,
Once echoed in laughter, now quietly confined.

Where paths twist and turn, the earth holds its breath,
Memories linger, enchanting in death.
With each cautious step, leaves murmur and sigh,
Footprints of time fade, like the last golden cry.

The canopy thickens, shadows blend with the dawn,
Once vibrant with life, now faded and drawn.
Yet still in the quiet, a flicker of grace,
Can be felt in the rustle, in this timeless place.

Misty breath lingers, as the morning awakes,
Each trail of forgotten, the heart gently takes.
Nature's sweet echoing whispers our fate,
For in every lost footfall, there lies something great.

Through the silence we walk, with presence and mind,
Binding our stories with those left behind.
For every lost journey, each shadow we trace,
Is woven in nature's embracing embrace.

Reflections of Twilight in the Leafy Veil

The sun dips low, a glowing ray,
Through leaves that dance at the end of day.
Shadows stretch long on the forest floor,
Whispers of night as they softly soar.

Colors blend in a warm embrace,
Nature's beauty, a gentle grace.
Golden hues fade to shades of gray,
Wishful thoughts drift quietly away.

Birds take flight, in the twilight's song,
Where dreams and daylight no longer belong.
Each moment captured in fading light,
Reflections whisper of tranquil night.

Stars begin to blink with delight,
The moon ascends, a beacon bright.
In the leafy veil, secrets lie,
As the world surrenders to the sky.

Softly wrapped in a night-time sigh,
Where echoes of wonder gently fly.
Fragrant breezes on an evening quest,
Inviting hearts to find their rest.

A Quiet Revelry in the Shade of Bark

Beneath the trees, a gathering cheer,
Where laughter dances, free from fear.
The sunlight filters through branches wide,
Inviting joys that the heart can't hide.

With cups raised high, sweet nectar shared,
In nature's arms, we feel ensnared.
Rustling leaves whisper secrets untold,
In this woodland realm, warm and bold.

The breeze carries stories of old,
Of dreams woven in the night's fold.
Children laughing, their spirits bright,
As shadows play in the fading light.

Bark wrapped trunks with mossy decor,
Hold memories of each laugh and roar.
In the shade, we lose track of time,
Each heartbeat a note of simple rhyme.

Echoing joy as twilight begins,
In this sanctuary, life always wins.
Grateful hearts under stars above,
In the quiet revelry, we find love.

Mysteries Concealed in Flickering Glimmers

Amidst the dusk, where shadows mix,
Lies a world woven with magical tricks.
Flickers of light in a hushed embrace,
A dance of secrets time can't erase.

Glimmers hide whispers of tales untold,
In moonlit frames, both young and old.
Every flicker, a promise that glows,
Filling the night with poetic prose.

The soft chirps of crickets play on repeat,
Their cadence synced with heartbeats sweet.
Nature's songs fill the air with dreams,
As the world shimmers in silver beams.

In the stillness, mysteries thrive,
A glimpse of magic that keeps us alive.
In the flickering glimmers, we find our way,
Through the unseen path at the end of day.

Secrets whirl in the cool night air,
Inviting the curious with gentle care.
In shadows deep, let your spirit soar,
For mysteries await on this enchanted shore.

Nature's Soft Whispers in the Hushed Grove

Enter the grove where silence reigns,
Where nature's song entangles the chains.
Soft whispers float through the leafy boughs,
A tranquil peace that nature endows.

The rustle of leaves tells an ancient tale,
In a symphony where spirits prevail.
Gentle winds brush against the skin,
While time stands still, invite peace within.

Birds hush their calls, an echo of grace,
In the heart of the grove, a sacred place.
Every sigh of the forest a verse,
Woven in mystery, a wondrous universe.

The ground beneath cradles stories deep,
In roots entwined, where memories sleep.
Nature hums soft, a lullaby sweet,
As wanderers pause in the choir of feet.

In the hush, let your worries cease,
Feel the embrace of nature's peace.
Nature's soft whispers wrap around,
In the grove where the heart is found.

Traces of Delight in Forgotten Vistas

In shadows deep where whispers dance,
Fleeting joy in a soft glance.
Colors fade, yet hearts embrace,
Lost in time's gentle grace.

Memories etched in golden light,
Hearts alight with pure delight.
Pathways worn by wandering feet,
Echoes of love in moments sweet.

In quiet glades, the laughter sneaks,
Amidst the trees, a secret speaks.
Nature cradles, softly binds,
With every breeze, the past unwinds.

Underneath the sprawling sky,
Colors blend as dreams comply.
Through the mist, the heart will soar,
Finding peace on forgotten shores.

So here's to joy, in silence blessed,
In traces where our souls find rest.
With every step on ancient land,
We uncover the dreams once planned.

Harmonizing with the Quietus of Nature

In the stillness, rhythms call,
Nature's voices softly fall.
Every leaf a gentle tune,
Underneath the watchful moon.

Rivers hum a sacred song,
With whispers where the stones belong.
Mountains echo, firm and wise,
Embracing clouds in tranquil skies.

The gentle rustle of the trees,
Carries secrets on the breeze.
As shadows play, the world stands still,
In harmony with nature's will.

Petals drift on zephyr's sigh,
Painting colors, low and high.
In every moment, peace we find,
In the quiet, hearts aligned.

So let us walk where silence reigns,
In nature's arms, release our chains.
With every breath, in still delight,
We dance with stars in velvet night.

The Hidden Sagas of Sunlit Woods

Beneath the boughs, the stories weave,
Of ancient tales we dare believe.
In sunlit glades, where shadows play,
Whispers linger, night and day.

Each tree a tome, each leaf a page,
Chronicling life's endless stage.
Creatures roam, each journey spun,
In the warmth of a waking sun.

Mossy carpets, soft and deep,
Guarding secrets that trees keep.
The laughter of the brook flows free,
Carrying tales of what will be.

In twilight's glow, the stories blend,
Magic lingers around each bend.
Through tangled roots and winding trails,
The woods reveal their timeless tales.

So wander slow in nature's book,
Discover wonders where we look.
In every twist, a life begun,
In the woods, we are all one.

Fables Carved in the Ancient Bark

In grooves of wood, the tales reside,
Of timeless wisdom, deep and wide.
Each notch a whisper of years gone by,
In the heartbeat of the earth, we sigh.

Stories known to stone and tree,
Where nature speaks so tenderly.
The winds carry legends, soft yet strong,
In the echoes, we find where we belong.

Twisted roots that grasp the ground,
With every creak, a truth is found.
A history carved through seasons' flow,
In rings of age, the past will show.

Old barks shelter life's embrace,
Holding memories in a quiet space.
The forest breathes, a sacred ark,
Guarding fables in every mark.

So pause and listen, let it spark,
The stories whispered in the dark.
In the ancient woods, love and strife,
Forge the fables that shape our life.

www.ingramcontent.com/pod-product-compliance
Ingram Content Group UK Ltd.
Pitfield, Milton Keynes, MK11 3LW, UK
UKHW021430160125
4146UKWH00006B/58